A Beginners Guide to Making a Million:

16 Golden Money Secrets to Becoming a Millionaire

Michael Cheung

A Beginners Guide to Making a Million:

16 Golden Money Secrets to Becoming a Millionaire

First Edition published by ALLYSKY LIMITED 2012

Copyright © Michael M. K. Cheung 2012

The author has asserted his moral right to be identified as the author of this work in accordance with the Copyrights, Designs and Patents Act 1988

All rights reserved under international and Pan-American Copyright Conventions. By payment of the required fees, you have been granted the non-exclusive rights to access and read the text of this book. No part of this text may be reproduced, transmitted, downloaded, decompiled, reverse engineered, or stored in any information storage and retrieval system, in any form or by any means whether electronic or mechanical, now known or hereinafter invented, without the express written permission of Michael M. K. Cheung and ALLYSKY Limited.

ISBN-13: 978-1481984881
ISBN-10: 1481984888

Limit of Liability/Disclaimer of Warranty: While the Publisher and Author have used their best efforts in preparing this book, they make no representations or warranties with respects to the accuracy or completeness of the contents of this book and specifically disclaim any implied warranties of merchantability or fitness for a particular purpose. No Warranty may be created or extended by sales representatives or written sales materials. The advice and strategies contained herein may not be suitable for your situation. You should consult with a professional where appropriate. Neither the publisher nor the Author shall be liable for any loss of profit or any other commercial damages, including but not limited to special, incidental, consequential, or other damages.

Names, characters, businesses, places, events and incidents are either the products of the author's imagination or used in a fictitious manner. Any resemblance to actual persons, living or dead, or actual events is purely coincidental.

TABLE OF CONTENTS

Preface 1

Lesson 1: How to grow a mighty oak from an acorn – The Miracle of Compounding 5

Lesson 2: Knowing what Seeds to Plant – The Asset Classes 15

Lesson 3: How do you feel about tomatoes? – Know yourself and risk 19

Lesson 4: Sipping pina colada's under a palm tree – Build Your Retirement Plan 25

Lesson 5: Your Broker shouldn't make you broke – Opening an investment account 35

Lesson 6: Buying good quality Seeds – Intelligent investing for smart people 39

Lesson 7: Don't keep all your eggs in one basket – Asset allocation and risk management 49

Lesson 8: Enjoying your money – How to spend it and have fun safely 55

Conclusion 59

Preface

A Beginners Guide to Making a Million: 16 Golden Money Secrets to Becoming a Millionaire is not just another investment book.

This book will take you on a journey through the investment world and can be read by anyone who has little or no knowledge of investments. All that is required is a keen mind and a free afternoon with a coffee in hand.

This guide will take you through the world of investing using as little maths as possible, but will still give you the tools and techniques needed to enable you to make great investment decisions.

This book will use lots of common sense and may be filled with some gardening stories, but the information and knowledge will be just as useful to you even if you don't have a potted plant.

Most people who begin to investigate and learn a new subject generally find themselves lost in a fog of technical terms, where the author has left the reader behind. In this book we promise to make sure all technical terms are explained as clearly as possible, so that once you have finished reading you will be able to understand how to look at the market and make sense of it all.

Why did we choose gardening as the theme for this book? There are a few good reasons why gardening is a useful tool for talking about financial investing. Firstly, Mother Nature is a great teacher of how things work and it is something that all

Michael M. K. Cheung

of us can visualize in our mind as a common point of reference. The powerful concepts that we will be giving you will have their roots planted in the old knowledge taught by a rice farmer to his son.

When you have finished reading this book you will understand how to grow your money, from a small seedling into a big oak tree. You will know what different kinds of investment are out there for you to put your money to work. You will be able to understand why most beginner investors lose their money to critters in the financial garden in less than a year and what to look out for. You will be all set to relax, sipping that pina colada under your very own palm tree.

The last thing this guide will show you is how to enjoy your money when that money tree is providing that cool shade for you to enjoy life's rich pleasures.

Michael M. K. Cheung

London

A Beginners Guide to Making a Million

Michael M. K. Cheung

A Beginners Guide to Making a Million

Lesson 1: How to grow a mighty oak from an acorn –The Miracle of Compounding

The single biggest lesson in how to become rich is – don't eat the seeds! Most people who are poor and are look at retiring with little or no money are in that situation because they have eaten the seeds. To grow a mighty oak tree you need to start with having that small acorn seed. Now the first exercise that I want you to do is go on the internet and Google 'acorn seed' and you will find a couple of nice images of acorns. The second exercise I want you to do is to go onto the Internet and Google Oak tree. Now you will see a BIG different between the two. The thing that surprised me was how small that little acorn seed is and how mighty and big that oak tree is. It's not something people often think about or focus on, but a quote came to mind that really said it well.

Zechariah 4:10 New Living Translation (NLT)

"Do not despise these small beginnings, for the LORD rejoices to see the work begin, to see the plumb line in Zerubbabel's hand."

Secret No 1: - Do not despise these small beginnings.

How many times have you thought I can't be bothered with investing my money as I only have $10 and I'm never going to get rich off that! Well my friend, that $10, is the acorn that, given enough time, care and attention will grow into the mighty oak tree that you have just Goggled.

Now I am not going to be quoting from the bible all the time, but there is a lot of wisdom in that book.

The second biggest lesson in how to become rich is – don't eat the shoots! The second problem people have is that after planting the seed i.e. that $10 into their savings account, they start to see good things like interest on their money which is the point where the acorn has germinated and now has a few leaves.

I found a great picture of an Oak Tree Sapling on about.com
http://forestry.about.com/od/treeplanting/p/oak_acorn.htm

Now, the problem is that people like to spend money and before that oak tree sapling can get to be an oak tree most people have pulled it out from the ground and eaten it! There is no seed, no sapling and no oak tree.

SECRET No 2:– Best to leave that Oak sapling alone if you want to see it grow into an oak tree.

Watering your tree on a regular basis is important if you want your oak sapling to grow into a mighty oak tree which will help it to grow nice and tall. This means putting money into your investment account on a regular basis. Whenever you have spare money you should put that into your saving account, but resist the urge to take any money out, as you will be restricting your sapling's growth.

Now I am going to change the scene and will introduce you to Rachel and Tom, our twenty year old investors. Here we will be looking at the 8th wonder of the world.

"Compound interest is the eighth wonder of the world. He, who understands it, earns it ... he who doesn't ... pays it."

A Beginners Guide to Making a Million

Quote - Albert Einstein

SECRET No 3:- Make compound interest work for you otherwise you will work for it.

Compound interest is when you earn interest on interest. So for example: If you have $100 and you get 10% interest then you have $100 x 1.10 = $110. Your principle or starting amount was $100 and you earned $10 interest in your first year. The second year you earned interest on the total amount i.e. $110 x 1.10 = $121 which is where the compounding miracle effect becomes apparent.

In Year two you now have earned $21 and as your earn interest on that interest you money grows very quickly. In 7 Years you would have doubled your money and your account would be worth $194.87.

Ok, now I want to take you back to Rachel and Tom.

Year 1:

Rachel is 20 years old and she works through the month and when she pays her bills and at the end of that month she has $100 left over. Instead of planting that seed money she spends it on the latest outfits, therefore eating her money seed in the process.

Her investment account remains at $0

Now 20 year old Tom also has $100 left over after working and paying his bills but instead of eating his seed money he plants it and put it into his investment account.

Michael M. K. Cheung

His investment is now at $100

At the moment there isn't much different between Rachel and Tom both are young and having a good time. Their quality of life has no significant differences.

Now Tom consistently waters that seed by putting that $100 away and at the end of the year he has saved $1200.

Rachel on the other hand has spent every month seed of $100 on outfits and has nothing in her saving account.

All is not lost for Rachel as those outfits that she bought are now her assets and can be sold on an online auction for a total of $120.

If she had saved her money she would have $1200 like Tom, but all she has is $120 worth of outfits.

She has an asset which if sold would return $120. This means that because her original spend on outfits was $1200 and the value is now $120 , the asset has lost a total value of $1200-$120 = $1080. So these assets have depreciated by 90% i.e. $1080/$1200 = 90%.

In Year 2:

Tom has earned 10% interest on his $1200 in his saving account. So he now has $1200x1.10=$1320. At the end of year two he has have another $1200 so he has a total of $1320+$1200 = $2520 and he also gets paid interest on his account, so he now has $2520 * 1.10 = $2772.

On the other hand Rachel has continued to buy outfits and

A Beginners Guide to Making a Million

eats out with the girls. She has saved nothing and her investment account is now at $0, whereas Tom's account now has $2772.

You can see that the difference is starting to get wider as the years progress.

Fast forward ten years...

Tom now has $21,037.40 and below you can see how his money grew over ten years.

http://www.thecalculatorsite.com/finance/calculators/compoundinterestcalculator.php#results

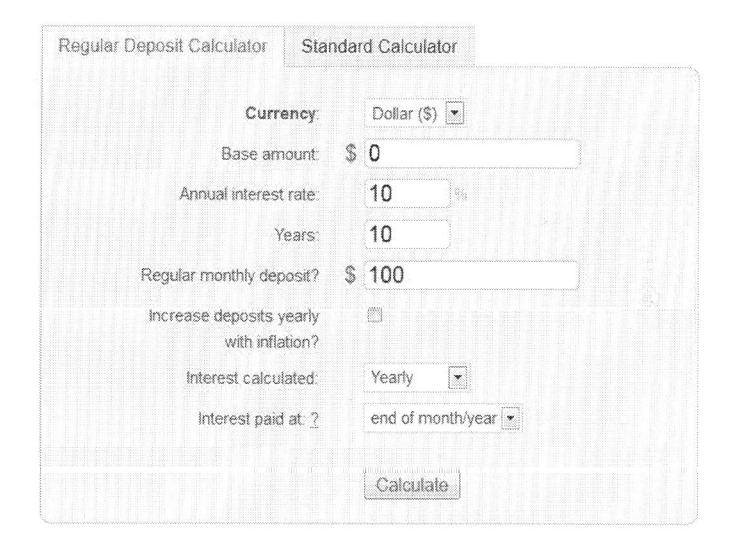

Regular Deposit Calculator	Standard Calculator
Currency:	Dollar ($)
Base amount:	$ 0
Annual interest rate:	10
Years:	10
Regular monthly deposit?	$ 100
Increase deposits yearly with inflation?	☐
Interest calculated:	Yearly
Interest paid at: ?	end of month/year
	Calculate

Michael M. K. Cheung

(interest calculated **yearly** - added at the end of each year)

Year	Year Deposits	Total Deposits	Year Interest	Total Interest	Total Sum
1	$ 1,200.00	$ 1,200.00	$ 120.00	$ 120.00	$ 1,320.00
2	$ 1,200.00	$ 2,400.00	$ 252.00	$ 372.00	$ 2,772.00
3	$ 1,200.00	$ 3,600.00	$ 397.20	$ 769.20	$ 4,369.20
4	$ 1,200.00	$ 4,800.00	$ 556.92	$ 1,326.12	$ 6,126.12
5	$ 1,200.00	$ 6,000.00	$ 732.61	$ 2,058.73	$ 8,058.73
6	$ 1,200.00	$ 7,200.00	$ 925.87	$ 2,984.61	$ 10,184.61
7	$ 1,200.00	$ 8,400.00	$ 1,138.46	$ 4,123.07	$ 12,523.07
8	$ 1,200.00	$ 9,600.00	$ 1,372.31	$ 5,495.37	$ 15,095.37
9	$ 1,200.00	$ 10,800.00	$ 1,629.54	$ 7,124.91	$ 17,924.91
10	$ 1,200.00	$ 12,000.00	$ 1,912.49	$ 9,037.40	$ 21,037.40

Base amount: $0.00
Interest: 10%
Years: 10

Regular Deposit Calculation

Rachel Account is shown below:

Year	Saving Account
1	$0.00
2	$0.00
2	$0.00
3	$0.00
4	$0.00
5	$0.00
6	$0.00
7	$0.00
8	$0.00
9	$0.00
10	$0.00

You can now see that after 10 years there is a BIG different between Rachel's and Tom's investment account's.

In Tom's case he has money working for him i.e. money literally making money, it's like having another job where you are making money while you are sleeping.

A Beginners Guide to Making a Million

In Rachel's case her outfits have the reverse effect. She needs to dry clean each item, which costs money. As her collection grows she also has to hire some storage, as she no longer has any space for them. Her assets are now costing her money instead of making her money.

The roles could have easily been reversed and Tom could have been the one who had no money and Rachel could have been the smart one. It is all about making small choices that will add up in a big way.

Remember:

Secret No 1: - Do not despise these small beginnings.

Let's project those numbers out to retirement age, to see what Tom's saving potential is. Tom has been saving and investing for 45 Years, since he was 20 and Rachel has spent all her money.

Again using this wonderful calculator
http://www.thecalculatorsite.com/finance/calculators/compoundinterestcalculator.php#results

Michael M. K. Cheung

| Regular Deposit Calculator | Standard Calculator |

Currency: Dollar ($)
Base amount: $ 0
Annual interest rate: 10 %
Years: 45
Regular monthly deposit? $ 100
Increase deposits yearly with inflation? ☐
Interest calculated: Yearly
Interest paid at: ? end of month/year

Calculate

Calculation results **Graph of results**

(interest calculated **yearly** - added at the end of each year)

Year	Year Deposits	Total Deposits	Year Interest	Total Interest	Total Sum
40	$ 1,200.00	$ 48,000.00	$ 53,111.11	$ 536,222.17	$ 584,222.17
41	$ 1,200.00	$ 49,200.00	$ 58,542.22	$ 594,764.39	$ 643,964.39
42	$ 1,200.00	$ 50,400.00	$ 64,516.44	$ 659,280.83	$ 709,680.83
43	$ 1,200.00	$ 51,600.00	$ 71,088.08	$ 730,368.91	$ 781,968.91
44	$ 1,200.00	$ 52,800.00	$ 78,316.89	$ 808,685.80	$ 861,485.80
45	$ 1,200.00	$ 54,000.00	$ 86,268.58	$ 894,954.38	$ 948,954.38

Base amount: $0.00
Interest: 10%
Years: 45

Regular Deposit Calculation

You can see that Tom now has $948,954.38 in his account. He put away $54,000 of his own money over 45 years. He received $86,268.58 interest per year on his money and has earned a whopping $894,954.38 of total interest due to the miracle of compound interest! This is why Albert Einstein called it the Eighth wonder of the world.

A Beginners Guide to Making a Million

You can now see how an acorn can grow into a mighty oak when left alone and watered and looked after.

Rachel has spent $1200 over 45 years so she has blown $54K of her money and has also lost out on the chance to earn $894,954.38 worth of interest on her money over 45 years. She won't be able to enjoy $86,268.58 interest per year on her money.

That is the price of making a small sacrifice and choosing to save $100 every month over 45 years. Now you can see the BIG difference that has happened over time when Tom has saved his money but Rachel has blown hers.

I like to remind the reader of this once more:

Remember:

Secret No 1: - Do not despise these small beginnings.

Michael M. K. Cheung

Lesson 2: Knowing what Seeds to Plant – The Asset Classes

In the garden there are many types of crop that can be planted, from apple trees to carrots and lettuce. Each crop has a different set of uses in the garden, for example apples trees are useful because once they are planted and have reached maturity they provide yearly crops of apples from then onwards. However it takes time for the apple trees to grow into maturity, so what are you going to eat while you are waiting for the tree to produce apples?

Well you might like to have a crop that grows quickly and can be harvested in less than a few months. It usually takes about 2 to 3 months for lettuce to grow from seed to harvest time! So, what has this all got to do with investing?

Well investment asset classes are just like choosing crops to grow in your garden. Each asset has a set of particular characteristics that serve a purpose and should be chosen to compliment your current needs.

The broad asset classes are as follows:

- Equities (stocks) e.g. US Stocks, International and emerging markets.

- Fixed-income (bonds)

- Cash equivalents, Deposit account with interest

- Real estate e.g. commercial and residential

- Commodities e.g. Precious metals, Agriculture and Energy

Michael M. K. Cheung

Fixed income is income investments that will pay interest on a regular basis, which can be yearly and will promise to pay your principle at maturity. Principle being your original investment amount.

In this analogy we can see that fixed income investments are very similar to purchasing a mature apple tree i.e. every year you can expect to have fruit and a good yield at that.

So an example of a fixed-income security would be a 5% fixed-rate government bond (Treasury Bonds) where a $2,000 investment would result in an annual $100 payment until maturity when the investor would receive the $2,000 back. But you should be aware that the price you pay for the guaranteed income is a lower rate of interest.

United States Treasury Inflation protected securities (TIPS), are a good way to get access to fixed income that also provide protection against inflation, so they are worth looking into.

Deposit accounts with interest are more like planting lettuce - you can very quickly get access to your money and earn interest, but it won't feed you for very long once you have spent all the money i.e. eaten all your money in your deposit account.

Equities provide you with a chance to purchase a part of a company. When you buy one share of a company that makes you a part owner of the company, and your percentage ownership is the number of shares you own divided by the number of shares that company has issued.

For example if XYZ Company had 200 shares issued and you

A Beginners Guide to Making a Million

own 1 share then you have 1/200 ownership of that company which is (1/200)*100=0.5% of the company. So you own half a percent of XYZ Company.

Now if that company made a profit of $10,000 for the year then you would receive a share of that profit which would be $10,000 * 0.5% = $50 for the year.

This would be issued as a dividend to you at the end of the financial year, either electronically to your broker account or by the old fashion way of the check.

Real Estate is property consisting of land and the buildings on it, along with its natural resources such as crops, minerals and water etc. You can participate in real estate either by buying the physical property or a financial instrument called a REIT.

REITs stand for Real Estate Investment Trust and they allow you to gain access to own a part of a set of buildings and apartments. This is factional ownership of say, the local shopping mall. For example if a ABC REIT had $5 Million and bought the local shopping mall then as a purchaser of one share in ABC REIT you would own a very small part of that mall through ownership of the REIT company.   If the mall was providing a $400,000 worth of profit through rental income then you would be entitled to a share of that profit and it would be issued to you accordingly. This can be quarterly or yearly. For example: **Acadia Realty Trust is traded on** (NYSE: AKR) have a dividend yield of about 2.8% and have been paying out quarterly since 1993.

Commodities represent physical resources such as Light

Crude Oil, Silver, Gold, Corn, Soybeans, Lean Hogs, Cocoa, Orange Juice and Sugar.

They are split up into areas, such as energy, metals, Agriculture, Livestock and Consumer.

Access to these commodities can be gained by buying an ETF, which is an Exchange Traded Fund. An investor would buy a share from an Exchange Traded Fund such as iShares Silver Trust, which trades under the code SLV on NYSE Arca.

The Trust holds silver bullion and is designed to provide investors with a simple and cost-effective method to gain exposure to the price of silver.

An investor might look to buy gold using an ETF such as SPDR Gold Shares and (ETFs) managed and marketed by State Street Global Advisors.

There are a few important things to note about buying ETFs. The first thing that you should know is that you are not buying a company that engages in gold or silver mining, such as Rio Tinto. You are actually buying a financial instrument that will track the underlying asset. So if the gold price doubles then your ETF will roughly double in value, but it won't track it perfectly as the ETF is a financial instrument and not the actual physical item i.e. it is not gold. However ETF generally perform their role very nicely and you don't have to worry about storing gold in a vault.

Lesson 3: How do you feel about tomatoes? – Know yourself and risk

An important question that investors should ask themselves is how they feel about risk. This question is important because the market can offer many types of ways to invest, but each option has varying levels of risk. This is a key factor in whether you are able to successfully make use of that particular option.

Think about our gardening example again. Now some gardeners are happy to grow apple trees because they know and understand the risk involved with growing and looking after apple trees. They know what critters to look out for so they can keep the trees healthy and they feel confident that they can monitor any signs of ill health or disease that the trees may show.

Other gardeners may feel happier about growing lettuce indoors where they are protected from frost and bugs. It is important to look at your ability to deal with risk personally and financially.

Buying individual shares in companies is going to be much more risky than investing in government bonds, which are backed by Uncle SAM. Normally one will find that the more risky the investment is the better the return is so, for example, a high flying startup technology stock might return 10 times your money in price appreciation but you could also lose all your money if the company failed.

If you bought a Treasury bond you might get 5% return on

your money over the year but you are very unlikely to lose your money, as it is backed by the US government.

When you buy shares in an individual company you are going to have to be active in monitoring the health of that company. You are going to have to read the quarterly reports. Companies have to report their financial situation quarterly in the form of a SEC Filing (Securities and Exchange Commission). This is done using a Form called 10-Q. 10-Q are done three times i.e. every 3 months and the final one appears in the yearly report which is called the 10-K. 10-K is the annual report which is a comprehensive summary of the public companies performance.

For example to find their quarterly reports 10-Q for intel you can go to their website

http://www.intc.com/sec.cfm?DocType=Quarterly

To look at their 10-K Annual Report you can look at the link below:

http://www.intc.com/annuals.cfm

Reading these reports is vital because once you buy a share in that company such as intel then you have become a part owner of that business. As an owner of the business it is in your best interest to look at how well that business is doing i.e. monitor for signs of disease and illness just like the apple tree owner does by looking at the leaves of his tree to see signs of disease. The business owner does this by looking at the 10-Q each 3 months and the 10-K at the end of the year.

A Beginners Guide to Making a Million

However some people find that this is too much hard work and they might decide to take less risk and buy Treasury Bonds that don't need you to keep reading those 10-Q and 10-K Reports. You might find that you are just not cut out to be an active business owner and that the risk of losing money is too much for you to bear.

Why does risk affect how successfully we are able to make money? The investor who cannot stomach risk will tend to buy when the company stock is going up and everyone is buying that stock, but he will also sell when it has dropped dramatically. This is very much like an apple tree owner who is buying more and more trees and planting an orchard and then when things go badly and he sees a little bit of disease on a few apples from his wonderful trees he start to rip up and throw away all the apples, including the good ones, in his panic.

People who are better at handling risk will make better decision when an apple starts to go bad and instead of throwing them all away in a mad panic they tend to keep calm and slowly remove the ones that have disease without throwing out the good ones in the process.

The really smart investors will not focus on all the ups and downs of the market but will choose to make wise purchases from the start. There are literally hundreds of companies out there and far more than the amount of money you have available to invest. This means that if you want to be successful you need to choose wisely and only cherry pick the best ones from the hundreds that are out there.

Michael M. K. Cheung

In the lifetime of an investor in the market there will be many ups and down that are caused by panics, manias, recession, crashes, booms, bubbles, corrections and busts. Each face of the market will drive greed and fear in the hearts of many of the investors. It will expose any character defects that you might have, for example you think that you can handle risk and have put all of your life savings in tech stocks. When the tech sector crashes will you be able to wake up in the morning and not feel terrible that you have lost 90 percent of your money?

Remember our garden story? Imagine if you didn't know the potential effects of weather on your crops. What would you do if you had invested all of your money in corn crop and a drought hit? It is better to invest in a variety of crops that can weather many types of market conditions. You see, it really is better to keep your eggs in many, separate baskets.

There are people who are so impatient to eat the apples from their orchards that they attempt to speed up the process by adding too much fertilizer and water and end up killing their trees. How does this relate to our investor? Well there is the issue of over commitment. They want to make their money grow faster so they use what is called leverage. Leverage is the financial version of fertilizer. It can certainly make your money grow but at the same time it can also kill your portfolio if you over use it.

How does leverage come about in investing? The usual form in which it appears is in buying a financial product that gives you 2 times or 3 times the movement of that instrument, for example. Leverage silver ETF would double your money

A Beginners Guide to Making a Million

when the underlying silver price moves 50%.

Example of a leverage contract: ETFS Leveraged Silver (LSIL) will change daily by 200% the daily percentage change in the DJ-UBS Silver Sub-IndexSM

Now leverage can be a good thing if used in small measures, but again you have to be very careful, as it is powerful stuff.

Michael M. K. Cheung

A Beginners Guide to Making a Million

Lesson 4: Sipping pina colada's under a palm tree – Build Your Retirement Plan

How do you go about building your retirement plan?

Planning for retirement can be confusing but it is one of the most important tasks that you will have to deal with for your financial security. The longer you leave it the harder it gets because there is less time for compound interest to work in your favor. Take for example the case where Doug starts saving for retirement at 20 years of age and retires at 65, he put away $100 a month. How much money would he have?

Calculation results   Graph of results

(interest calculated **yearly** - added at the end of each year)

Year	Year Deposits	Total Deposits	Year Interest	Total Interest	Total Sum
40	$ 1,200.00	$ 48,000.00	$ 53,111.11	$ 536,222.17	$ 584,222.17
41	$ 1,200.00	$ 49,200.00	$ 58,542.22	$ 594,764.39	$ 643,964.39
42	$ 1,200.00	$ 50,400.00	$ 64,516.44	$ 659,280.83	$ 709,680.83
43	$ 1,200.00	$ 51,600.00	$ 71,088.08	$ 730,368.91	$ 781,968.91
44	$ 1,200.00	$ 52,800.00	$ 78,316.89	$ 808,685.80	$ 861,485.80
45	$ 1,200.00	$ 54,000.00	$ 86,268.58	$ 894,954.38	$ 948,954.38

Base amount: $0.00
Interest: 10%
Years: 45

Regular Deposit
Calculation

Our earlier calculations show the results. Doug would have $948,954.38 available in his retirement account.

What would be the effect if Doug had decided to hold back on starting his retirement plan until he was 30 years old because he wanted to travel the world and was too busy thinking about other things?

Doug would have started at 30 years old and retired at 65 which give him 35 years to invest his money at 10% interest per year and if he was putting away $100 a month i.e. $1200 a year. He would have $357,752.17 in his retirement account.

Now if you divided $948,954.38 by $357,752.17 you can see how much better off Doug would be by starting in his twenties.

$948,954.38/$357,752.17=2.65

So basically Doug would be 2.65 times better or in absolute money terms;

$948,954.38-$357,752.17 = $591,202.21

Calculation results | Graph of results

(interest calculated **yearly** - added at the end of each year)

Year	Year Deposits	Total Deposits	Year Interest	Total Interest	Total Sum
30	$ 1,200.00	$ 36,000.00	$ 19,739.28	$ 181,132.11	$ 217,132.11
31	$ 1,200.00	$ 37,200.00	$ 21,833.21	$ 202,965.32	$ 240,165.32
32	$ 1,200.00	$ 38,400.00	$ 24,136.53	$ 227,101.85	$ 265,501.85
33	$ 1,200.00	$ 39,600.00	$ 26,670.19	$ 253,772.04	$ 293,372.04
34	$ 1,200.00	$ 40,800.00	$ 29,457.20	$ 283,229.24	$ 324,029.24
35	$ 1,200.00	$ 42,000.00	$ 32,522.92	$ 315,752.17	$ 357,752.17

Base amount: $0.00
Interest: 10%
Years: 35

Regular Deposit Calculation

So by starting 10 years earlier Doug would be $600,000 better off or 2.65 times better off!

You can see how compound interest needs time to work its

A Beginners Guide to Making a Million

magic in the same what that growing an apple seed needs time in order to grow into an apple orchard and then provide you with plenty of apples to eat year after year.

But it doesn't stop there. Now look at the interest that Doug would get had he started when he was twenty.

$86,268.58 a year income as interest and compare this with what he would receive if he started ten years later - $32,522.92!

Now I think you would like to have a yearly income of $86,268.58 instead of $32,522.92

This would equate to the difference between you being well off vs. having to go on a tidy budget to get by on $32,522.92

Let's just run some final numbers to see what Doug would have to do to catch up to creating a yearly income of $86,268.58.

How much money would Doug have to save each month if he started at 30 years of age to get the same yearly retirement income as if he started in his 20s?

Have a guess and then check the answer below:

Doug would need to save $265.5 a month instead of $100 if he wanted to play catch up with his younger self.

Now $165.5 extra is quite a bit of money and is more than twice what he would have to put away if he had started it earlier.

If Doug was earning $2000 a month then he would have to spend ($265.5/$2000)*100=13% of his income vs. ($100/$2000)*100=5% of his income. You can see that it is better for Doug to spend just 5 percent of his income and start at 20 years of age rather than start later and have to spend 13% of his income year in year out until he retired at 65. Doug would have to find that extra $165.5 a month for the next 35 years because he decided to start 10 years later in his thirties. You could buy a new Kindle Fire every month for that price for the next 35 years!

So the case is clear – You should start as soon as possible and put in the minimum of 5% of your income as a good starting point for getting your retirement plan off the ground.

Secret No 4: Start investing your money as soon as possible; the earlier the better.

A Beginners Guide to Making a Million

How much better off would Doug be if he decided to really go for it and put 10% of his income into his retirement plan. So he put in $200 a month instead of $100. Let's run those numbers and see what we get.

	Regular Deposit Calculator	Standard Calculator
Currency:	Dollar ($)	
Base amount:	$ 0	
Annual interest rate:	10	%
Years:	45	
Regular monthly deposit?	$ 200	
Increase deposits yearly with inflation?	☐	
Interest calculated:	Yearly	
Interest paid at: ?	end of month/year	

Calculate

Calculation results | Graph of results

(interest calculated **yearly** - added at the end of each year)

Year	Year Deposits	Total Deposits	Year Interest	Total Interest	Total Sum
40	$ 2,400.00	$ 96,000.00	$ 106,222.21	$ 1,072,444.35	$ 1,168,444.35
41	$ 2,400.00	$ 98,400.00	$ 117,084.43	$ 1,189,528.78	$ 1,287,928.78
42	$ 2,400.00	$ 100,800.00	$ 129,032.88	$ 1,318,561.66	$ 1,419,361.66
43	$ 2,400.00	$ 103,200.00	$ 142,176.17	$ 1,460,737.83	$ 1,563,937.83
44	$ 2,400.00	$ 105,600.00	$ 156,633.78	$ 1,617,371.61	$ 1,722,971.61
45	$ 2,400.00	$ 108,000.00	$ 172,537.16	$ 1,789,908.77	$ 1,897,908.77

Base amount: $0.00
Interest: 10%
Years: 45

Regular Deposit Calculation

We can see that by saving $200 a month that Doug has now

Michael M. K. Cheung

$1,897,908.77 in his retirement account.

He gets $172,537.16 worth of interest yearly from his retirement account.

He contributed a total of $108,000 of his own money over those 45 years.

If you were Doug could you live happily off $172,537.16?

So as the person who is looking to set up their golden years you should think can I afford to put in 10% of my income to retirement vs. 5 percent.

The difference is living comfortably well off vs. just being well off.

$172,537.16 income a year could certainly help to pay for a few nice holidays a year and a few nice meals!

So one key think to think about is how much money you want when you retire and using the 5% to 10% of your income rule and start saving as soon as possible is critical to that retirement plan.

Now that you have a good idea of how much money you need to save and what percentage of your income you should be looking at putting away, the question turns to what investment options do you have access to?

The government has put several investment schemes into place to help you when it comes to retirement.

They are as follows:

A Beginners Guide to Making a Million

- Traditional 401K

- Roth 401K

- Traditional IRA

- Roth IRA

401k plans are offered by employers. The employee chooses to have a portion of his or her paycheck deducted directly and put into the 401k plan. An employer may match this contribution so thereby double the amount that is put into the 401k plan.

Take for example Doug and his $2000 paycheck. Now if he put in 5% which is $100 a month his employer (if very generous) might match that like for like and also put in $100 thereby bringing his monthly contribution to $200.

Not all employers are that generous and you will need to check with your own employer to see how much they will match your contributions. You are also restricted to what investment you can make so you need to contact your employer 401k plan provider to see what investments are allowed.

Whilst inside the 401k plan the money will grow and compound tax free but once you get to the point of retirement you will have to start paying taxes on the income that you draw from your retirement plan.

There is one last point to consider about the 401k plan, which is access to your money. It is designed to be a long term investment vehicle, so if you want to get access to your money in an emergency then that is going to be an issue. There are tax penalties that are incurred when you try to get that money before your retire.

IRA. This is the Individual Retirement Account, which is self-managed and outside of your employer control. You have a greater choice of investment in an IRA vs. the 401K plan.

The basic tax advantage is the same in the IRA and the 401K however you need to know the following in 2012:

In the IRA the contributions are only fully tax deductible for people who have incomes below $58,000 (Single filers).

For married couples filing jointly and where the spouse contributing to the traditional IRA is covered by an employer-based retirement plan: $92,000 to $112,000.

The IRS has increased the amount you may contribute towards your 401(k) plan:

In the 2012 tax year you may contribute up to $17,000 ($500 more than in 2011) into their 401(k) plan.

In 2012 tax year the existing annual contribution limit of $5,000 apply your IRA and if you are over 50 then it is $6,000.

The difference between Roth and traditional is as follows:

Traditional IRA and 401K is where you put money in and it is pre-tax or tax deductible and then you get tax on the income that you get i.e. tax on the way out. But with Roth you pay into the scheme using after tax dollar but your money is tax

A Beginners Guide to Making a Million

free on the way out i.e. when you draw an income.

What you choose will depend on what is available to you and also your financial situation. If you want to save a few dollars today you can look at using pre-tax dollar but you will be taxed in the future where the tax rate is unknown i.e. when you draw your income. Who know what the tax rate is then!

Or you could pay taxes now and collect tax free later this is good if you have more money to spare and are happy to pay a few dollars more so that you can avoid the uncertainty of the tax rate later on when you come to collect.

It's really down to your preference.

Secret No 5: Compound your money tax FREE to earn as much money as possible.

With the 401K plan the employer is effectively offering you FREE money and that is a blessing. You should always take free money when it is offered to you and it will be like gasoline to fire when it comes to your retirement fund.

Secret No 6: Always say yes to FREE money!

You can get access to your money in your IRA whenever you want but you will face penalties, for example the traditional IRA will charge 10%. You can expect to start taking money out when you are 59.5 Years of age without getting penalties but check with your provider for the fine print details.

The same applies to your 401k plan again it is 59.5 years of age that you can get access to your money and by 70.5 you are forced to start using those funds.

Lesson 5: Your Broker shouldn't make you broke – Opening an investment account

You have a few choices to make

Choice No 1: The discount broker

You pay them when they execute your trade, for example you buy $1000 of IBM stock and your pay them $10 to execute that trade. This usually works for those that have the time and energy to make their own well informed decisions by looking at 10-K and 10-Q Report and knowing what to look for and how to interpret them.

You can go with a discount broker such as **E-Trade Financial Corporation** (NASDAQ: ETFC) or **Scottrade,** which is privately owned**.**

Both of these provide an online brokerage service, which is a straight forward way that you can manage your accounts.

Choice No 2: Mutual fund Account

Mutual funds are good for those who don't want to know about investment but still want their money working for them. They have good and bad points, which means that they work for some people and not for others.

You could look at using WELLS FARGO and open a mutual fund account online.

Example of a mutual fund is Schwab Total Stock Market Index Fund (SWTSX). This has a morning star rating of 4 out of 5. The fund generally invests at least 80% of its net assets in stocks that are included in The Dow Jones U.S

Their top ten holdings include:

Top 10 Holdings

Portfolio weighting

AAPL Apple Inc	3.69%
XOM Exxon Mobil Corporation	2.65%
T AT&T Inc	1.44%
MSFT Microsoft Corporation	1.43%
GE General Electric Co	1.43%
IBM International Business Machines Corp	1.40%
CVX Chevron Corp	1.40%
JNJ Johnson & Johnson	1.23%
PFE Pfizer Inc	1.17%
PG Procter & Gamble Co	1.15%

A Beginners Guide to Making a Million

Choice No 3: Full Service Brokerage Account

A full service broker will provide services such as retirement planning, tax preparation and strategies, research knowledge on stocks and bonds; most importantly you get access to certain private equity and hedge funds that might not be on offer from those discount brokers.

Full brokerages include:

Merrill Lynch and Morgan Stanley; these firms are like buying into the top of the range Mercedes car where you get all leather seat and cruise control and all the extras. Whatever you want they can cater for.

If you are famous and have lots of money then you might park all your money with the full brokerage guys and they will do everything for you. You just pick up the phone and talk to them from time to time to see what's going on and how much money you have made.

What can the average Joe do? Well if you don't have millions of dollars but you want to get rich then you have to trade something else in exchange.

SECRET No 7: Educate yourself about money and you will get rich faster!

Now if you educate yourself about the market and business and investment then you won't need to pay other people to tell you about those things. You will be able to make informed choices for yourself. If you have more time than money then that is what you are going to have to do when you are look at getting rich.

First learn to read the 10-Q report and the 10-K Report that are issued by companies. If you can read these reports then you can see if your tree is showing signs of disease and illness. For example if the company is showing that it is borrowing more money every year and its profits are getting smaller then you want to think about selling that company. You can only know about that if you read those reports, don't wait for other people to tell you about it. Educating yourself gives you an advantage over 90 percent of the other players who don't bother to read those reports.

Read the Wall Street Journal, read about how smart business people have made their money because once you understand how they operate you can see if your investments are good or not. As an owner of companies you really need to think like a business owner. After all it is YOUR company as you have shares (stock) in it.

SECRET No 8: Think like a business owner to get rich owning stocks

Lesson 6: Buying good quality Seeds – Intelligent investing for smart people

"Nowadays people know the price of everything and the value of nothing."

- Oscar Wilde

What has this got to do with investing?

Smart and intelligent investing is not about following the latest trend or tips from the talking heads on business and financial TV or even just reading the Wall Street Journal. It's not about knowing the price of each stock that makes up the Dow Jones or the S&P. Anyone one can tell you the price of a stock and list the components of a market index such as the Dow Jones, but what is much more difficult to do is to tell you the value of those stocks.

An average investor will look at the price of stocks in the financial paper and think if it is trading at $10 then that stock is cheap vs. a stock trading at $600. What represents better value, buying the $10 share of company A or buying a $600 share of company B?

Most people would answer it is better value to buy the $10 share of Company A because it is cheaper than the $600 share of company B. They would argue that they are getting one share at $10 vs. one share at $600. That logic does seem to make some kind of common sense. But it is not a good way to know the value of what we have purchased.

What we need is some kind of common yardstick that we can

use to compare Company A against Company B.

The smart intelligent investor would use what is called the max-min principle. Which is maximize the benefit but minimize the cost or outlay that is required to acquire that investment.

SECRET No 9: Minimize the cost but Maximize the benefit.

So first we need to define what the benefit to us is when we purchase an investment. The general benefit to having an investment is getting some income from owning that investment.

So for example, if I bought $1000 worth of Treasury Bonds and it paid $50 at the end of the year in terms of income then my return on my money would be ($50/$1000) x 100 = 5%

The return on my investment for the year is known as the yield.

If I bought a rental apartment for $100,000 and I rented it out and collected $3000 per year then the yield would be calculated as follows:

Yield = (Rental Income / Cost of Investment) * 100

Yield = ($3000/$100,000) * 100

Yield = 0.03 * 100

Yield = 3%

The yield i.e. your return on your investment, is the way that

A Beginners Guide to Making a Million

you can compare one investment against another.

Even though the investment amounts are different we were still able to compare one investment against another by looking at their respective yields.

So now we can answer the question of which investment is better?

The treasury bonds had a yield of 5% and the rental apartment has a yield of 3%.

So the better investment in this example is the Treasury bond that gave us a 5% yield.

We can see this even more clearly when we use the same amounts.

If we buy $100,000 of Treasury Bonds that give 5% yield, what is the income on our money?

Income Returned= Amount invested * (yield/100)

Income Returned= $100,000 * (yield/100)

Income Returned= $100,000 * (5/100)

Income Returned= $100,000 * 0.05

Income Returned= $5000

If we buy $100,000 rental apartment that gives 3% Yield, what is the income on our money?

Income Returned= Amount invested * Yield

Income Returned= $100,000 * (yield/100)

Income Returned= $100,000 * (3/100)

Income Returned= $100,000 * 0.03

Income Returned= $3000

Clearly we can see that the treasury bonds have returned $5000 compared to the $3000 returned by our rental apartment.

So the better investment in this example is the Treasury bond that gave us a 5% yield.

We can use the yield to compare other investment scenarios so for example take these two below:

Example 1:

Your friend asks you to put $10,000 in a pig farm and at the end of the year there are no profits.

Yield = (Income / Cost of Investment) * 100

Yield = 0 /$10,000 * 100

Yield = 0%

This would be a bad investment.

Example2:

You purchase a storage unit for $10,000 and rent it out for $50 per month.

A Beginners Guide to Making a Million

Yearly income = $50 * 12 months = $600 per Year

Yield = (Income / Cost of Investment) * 100

Yield = ($600 / $10,000) * 100

Yield = 0.06 * 100

Yield = 6%

The purchase of a storage unit is a good investment in this example because the yield is better.

It is better to get 6% yield on your money than it is to have 0% yield on your money.

The storage unit investment even outperformed the rental apartment, which gave us 3% yield and was still even better than the 5% we got on the Treasury Bonds.

Note: Details have been simplified somewhat because this does not take into account tax issues which would be a matter for you and your accountant to discuss.

However, these calculations will give you a great tool that you can use to compare different investments.

It doesn't matter if you are a property investor, fixed income investor or a stocks and shares investor.

These yield calculation formulas will serve you well.

Getting back to our stock situation Company A vs. Company B.

Well, it would seem Company A is better at $10 a share than Company B, which is $600 a share.

Now that you know about yields you can make an informed smart intelligent choice in the matter.

Looking up the yield for Company A in, say, the Wall Street Journal you find that it is paying a yield of 0%. This means that they didn't return any money to you at the end of the year in the way of profits.

Income Returned= Amount invested * (Yield/100)

Income Returned= $10x (0/100)

Income Returned= $0

So your $10 produced an income of $0

Now compare this to the $600 a share company B. Looking up the yield in the Wall Street Journal you find that it is paying 2% Yield.

Income Returned= Amount invested x (yield/100)

Income Returned= $600 x (2/100)

Income Returned= $600 x (0.02)

Income Returned= $12

From this calculation you can see that the better investment was Company B, which cost you $600 but paid your $12 income for the year. Even though the investment cost more in dollar terms, it was a BETTER investment when you looked at the income returned at the end of the year i.e. the Benefit to you.

There is another important point that you should know about with the yield formula.

Yield = (Income / Cost of Investment) * 100

As we reduce the cost of the investment we find that yield will increase.

Example:

A storage unit that costs $10,000 and pays $600 a year in rental income

Yield = ($600/$10,000)*100

Yield = 0.06 * 100

Yield = 6%

Now imagine if the storage unit owner was in a hurry to sell and sold the unit to you at the end of the year for $1000

Yield = ($600/$1000) * 100

Yield = 0.6 * 100

Yield = 60%

You would find that the yield had gone up by ten times!!!

$1000 investment now gives you $600 a year worth of rental income!

So just to recap, instead of paying $10,000 for that same investment you paid $1000. The yield dramatically rose from 6% to 60%. Nothing else changed except the price you paid!

SECRET No 10: Wait and be patient and only buy into an investment that gives you great yields.

SECRET No 11: The rich get rich by being very patient and buying at the best moment

SECRET No 12: Pay as little as possible for that same investment and always look at the yield value

SECRET No 13: The smart investor focuses on yield and not on the price

The smart investor focuses on the yield and not on the price, however be careful because investment that pays a high yield can also carry a lot of risk.

SECRET No 14: Watch the yield and look at the risk involved.

Investments that pay good yields can be great but also present a potential minefield.

For example:

A rental house that cost $25,000 and yields 10% i.e. $2,500 seems like a good deal until you find out that the house is in a poor neighborhood which is blighted by drug dealers and petty thieves.

A Company might have a high yield of 15% and also have a cheap share price but they are taking on a large bank loan to

A Beginners Guide to Making a Million

use for the purpose of paying out dividend profit at the end of the year. At this same time they are losing money because they are not selling enough goods to their customers. This company is going bust soon! Always read the 10-Q and 10-K before you buy into a company so that you can check on their health.

Michael M. K. Cheung

Lesson 7: Don't keep all your eggs in one basket – Asset allocation and risk management

Asset allocation is about deciding what kind of investments you are going to be putting your money to work in. Think about how a farmer goes about planting different crops so that there is always something to harvest throughout the year. He also makes sure that he plants crops that will be able to withstand various weather environments. The farmer will plant crops that are hardy so that they can resist bugs and dry weather seasons. A critical part of being a good investor is making sure you choose a good set of investments that can withstand various economic situations.

Diversification is the method that a farmer uses to spread his risk by planting various crops that have different characteristics. The investor uses the same method but instead of planting crops he chooses different investments.

However it is not just a matter of choosing different investments such as buying IBM and Microsoft because they are both technology stocks. You are not going to get much diversification by doing that. It is much like planting lettuces and cabbages. Both are going to have similar problems when it comes to slugs and snails eating their leaves. You need to think about diversifying so if you suffer from one problem, such as snails, it does not have to affect all of your crops. So the smart farmer would plant lettuce and also plant some apple trees that would be much more resistant to snails.

An investor going by this analogy would be looking to diversify by buying tech stocks and Gold ETFs because the gold market would give you some protection against the falling dollar, where as a falling dollar might have an negative impact on the price of the tech stocks.

So what does a diversified portfolio look like?

Portfolio No 1:

Well there is the Talmud Asset Allocation Model that you could use.

"Let every man divide his money into three parts, and invest a third in land, a third in business and a third let him keep by himself in reserve" – So it is written in the Talmud.

Asset Class No 1: Reserves (33.3%)

33.3% should be invested in cash and cash equivalents i .e. CDs, Bank Saving Account and saving bonds and Treasury Bills.

Asset Class No 2: Real Estate (33.3%)

This could be real estate investment via REITs, home property, commercial property, storage units and apartments and farmland.

Asset Class No 3: Businesses (33.3%)

This could be US stocks, international stocks and small private businesses.

If you had $450,000 in your portfolio, you could put $150,000 into cash reserves or T-Bills that earn 3%, $150,000 into real

A Beginners Guide to Making a Million

estate that earns 6%, and $150,000 into US equity i.e. businesses such as blue chip stocks.

Portfolio No 2:

There are many different portfolio models that you can look at. Another interesting one is the income portfolio model

10% saving accounts and money market accounts.

20% in US Dow or S&P 500 stocks that have yields of 3% to 6%

35% in real estate investment such as rental unit and storage units.

35% in Liquid Government bonds such as Treasury Bonds

Portfolio No 3:

Then there is a more balance portfolio that you might look at because it has a little bit of everything.

20% investment grade corporate and government bonds

10% US large capitalization blue chip stocks

10% Foreign large capitalization blue chip stocks

10% US small cap stocks

10% US midcap stocks

10% cash reserves

20% real estate

10% gold and silver

Depending on what you want to achieve with your money any of these portfolio examples will be a good starting point for further investigations. There is no right or wrong answer when it comes to creating a portfolio and a lot depends on your risk profile, how old you are and what the portfolio is designed to do.

Portfolio 3 is a great all-rounder for people of all ages.

Portfolio 1 is great for those who want to try the financial methods used by the Jewish people who follow the Talmud and they have definitely been very successful at business and investing.

Risk management is about buying and selling investments so that you manage the risk that is present in your portfolio. This allows you to minimize the amount of risk that you have. The first way to do this is to choose a portfolio where your money is spread across a number of assets that are not too heavily connected, so for example you don't put 10% in all US large cap tech stocks! Spread them around a bit by buying some of each sector, such as pharmaceuticals, tech, food and beverages and services etc.

The second thing that you can do is called rebalancing your portfolio; which means as your investment grows in one area and decreases in others then the percentage that you started with do not match the starting portfolio percentages any more. You need to rebalance them back to the original percentages.

A Beginners Guide to Making a Million

For example: Going back to our Talmud portfolio No 1

If the stock market crashed by 50% at the end of the first year, your account balances would be $154,500 in cash reserves, $159,000 in real estate, and $75,000 in stocks. Your total account balance would be $388,500, a loss of $61,500.

To rebalance this portfolio you would take $388,500 divided by 3

Which means $129,500 should go into each Asset Class.

$129,500 for cash

$129,500 for real estate

$129,500 for stocks

So you would reduce your cash from $154,500 to $129,500. Reduce some real estate to $129,500 from $159,000 and increase your stocks from $75,000 to $129,500 i.e. buy another $54,500 worth of stocks by taking that money from your cash and real estate.

Michael M. K. Cheung

Lesson 8: Enjoying your money – How to spend it and have fun safely

Now that you have made plenty of money does the story end there?

Getting rich is one thing but keeping it and staying rich is another thing and there are many people who have made lots of money and then lost it all again!

One secret to keeping all of that lovely money is to not spend it all. It doesn't matter whether you are a millionaire or even a billionaire. If you spend more than you earn consistently then you WILL go broke. We all know of a few famous rappers, entertainers, singers and sport stars that spent more than they earned and then went broke.

SECRET No 15: Spend less than your earn if you want to stay rich and avoid going broke

You should avoid having too many expensive running costs such as that lovely yacht, private jet or that Ferrari 250 GTO. These luxury items will eat you alive unless you really have enough income to service them.

Take for example a portfolio that is worth $1,000,000 and is throwing off 10% yield, which means you are earning $100,000. Now we are not going to use tax in our calculations for this example. Even though you could afford to buy a used Ferrari F430 Berlinetta at $245,500 how much would it cost you to run this car? Well a good ballpoint figure would be 10% of the cost of the car per year which means it is going to cost you around $24,500 to service it, replace tires and keep it from getting damaged etc. Now that is 24% of your pre-tax earnings. So even though you can afford to buy that Ferrari outright it will be eating away at your income and depreciating, as it gets older.

What you could do with your money is make sure you have paid off all of your personal debts, including credit cards and that outstanding mortgage debt on your house.

You should also look to buy or own a house that functionally serves you well so you might only need that 3 bedroom house instead of the 16 bedroom mansion with swimming pool and a driveway that parks 4 cars!

You might want to buy items when you need them rather than buying designer items because they have a status symbol attached to them. Once you start living with expensive items then you need to keep all your items at a similar standard, which can begin to get expensive once things break and wear out!

Even though you are making good money from your investment you should look to keep adding to them by building on them even more.

SECRET No 16: Don't spend the principle i.e. that $1,000,000 in your retirement account.

ONLY ever spend the interest that you earn

When spending your money always work on what is the value that you are getting for your money and this will keep you

A Beginners Guide to Making a Million

from wasting it on depreciating assets that cost you money to service.

Rich people always make sure their children know the value of money and so won't spend the family resources in a way that will put the principle at risk i.e. that $1,000,000 that you have saved.

When you see people spending $200,000 on cars they are either stupid and have spent all their earning and have no savings whatsoever or they are extremely rich and they are spending just a fraction of their income. We might be talking about a guy who has a net worth of $40 Million and earns 10% so that he would have $4 Million at his disposal each year and a $200,000 car is no problem for him as it is only 5 percent of his income for that year.

You could afford to buy at $2 Million mansion if your net worth was $40 Million. It would just be 5% of your asset base.

Michael M. K. Cheung

Conclusion

I hope that you have found this book to be a valuable read and that you will be able to put many of the money secrets to good use over the next 45 investment years that you have ahead of you. It doesn't matter if you are an absolute beginner or a season professional investor there is always something to learn about making money and investing wisely. Sometimes things make more sense when you have read through them twice or even three times. You might want to read through this book again and refer to it from time to time as you learn more about investing and how these lessons and secrets can be applied to making money.

It has been an honor for me that you have taken the time to read this far and I wish you great success in your investing, retirement plans and success in general. Good Luck.

Best wishes

Michael Cheung

You may also like to read my other book:

Sun Tzu the Art of Making Money: Strategies for getting through a tough economy

It is available for purchase on the Amazon website. You can also borrow it from the kindle owners' lending library if you have an Amazon prime member subscription and own a kindle device.

Made in the USA
Lexington, KY
08 February 2013